※ Smithsonian

DIGGING FOR TYRANNOSAURUS REX

BY THOMAS R. HOLTZ JR., Ph.D.

a Discovery

TIMELINE

CAPSTONE PRESS
a capstone imprint

Capstone Press
1710 Roe Crest Drive
North Mankato, Minnesota 56003
www.capstonepub.com

The name of the Smithsonian Institution and the sunburst logo are
registered trademarks of the Smithsonian Institution. For more
information, please visit www.si.edu.

Our very special thanks to Mike Brett-Surman, PhD, Museum Specialist for
Fossil Dinosaurs, Reptiles, Amphibians, and Fish at the National Museum of
Natural History, Smithsonian Institution, for his curatorial review. Capstone would
also like to thank Kealy Wilson, Product Development Manager, and the following
at Smithsonian Enterprises: Ellen Nanney, Licensing Manager; Brigid Ferraro,
Vice President, Education and Consumer Products; Carol LeBlanc,
Senior Vice President, Education and Consumer Products.

Library of Congress Cataloging-in-Publication Data
Holtz, Thomas R., 1965– author.
Digging for Tyrannosaurus rex : a discovery timeline / by Thomas R. Holtz, Jr.
pages cm.—(Smithsonian. Dinosaur discovery timelines)
Summary: "Provides an annotated timeline of the discovery of Tyrannosaurus rex
including details on the scientists, dig sites, fossils, and other findings that have
shaped our knowledge of this dinosaur"—Provided by publisher.
Audience: Ages 8–12.
Audience: Grade 2–6.
Includes bibliographical references and index.
ISBN 978-1-4914-2125-3 (library binding)
ISBN 978-1-4914-2366-0 (paperback)
ISBN 978-1-4914-7261-3 (ebook)
1. Tyrannosaurus rex—Juvenile literature. 2. Dinosaurs—Juvenile literature.
3. Paleontology—History—Juvenile literature. I. Title.
QE862.S3H6533 2015
567.912'9—dc23   2014024631

Printed in the United States of America, in North Mankato, Minnesota.
072015   009085R

Editorial Credits
Kristen Mohn, editor; Lori Bye and Aruna Rangarajan, designers; Kelly Garvin,
media researcher; Kathy McColley, production specialist

Photo Credits
Alamy: Lou Linwei, 26(top), Sergey Krasovskiy/Stocktrek Images, 17(top right),
Stephen Saks Photography, 18(right), SZ Photo/Scherl, 12(tr), The Natural History
Museum, 6(b); Corbis: 20 (bottom left), Gary Cameron, 19, Ken Gillespie, 9(tr),
Konstantin Mikhailov, 16(r), Layne Kennedy, 20(r), Louie Psihoyos, 18(bl),
22(left), Mark Stevenson/Stocktrek Images, 29, Ron Erwin/All Canada Photos,
5, Wong Maye-E/AP, 17(bl); Dreamstime/Cmindm, 21(left); Getty Images:
Science Photo Library/Mark Garlick, cover, Science Picture Co, 8(b), Hyoung
Chang, 22(r); Illustration by Erica Lyn Schmidt, 25; James Field, 23(l); Jon
Hughes, backcover, 1, 11(r), 23(r); Library of Congress: Detroit Publishing Co,
12(bl), Prints & Photographs Division, 7(br); National Geographic Creative/Xing
Lida, 27; Peabody Museum of Natural History, Yale University, 10(b); Photo
by Anne Weil, University of California Museum of Paleontology, 2014, http://
ucmp.berkeley.edu, 14(tr); Photo courtesy of Gregory M. Erickson, 21(tr); Photo
courtesy of Royal Tyrrell Museum, Drumheller, Alberta, 9(b); Photo courtesy of
Thomas Carr taken by Belinda Carr, 15(r); Science Source: Paul D. Stewart, 7(bl),
Shutterstock: DM7, 9(l), Catmando, 26(b); Superstock/Ambient Image Inc, 15(l);
Wikimedia: 7(t), 8(tr), AMNH, 13(l), Popular Science Monthly vol. 67, 10(tr),
R. Weber, 11(l), ScottRobertAnselmo, 14(bl), Stu Spivack, 24(r), William D.
Matthew, 12(br)

Table of Contents

TYRANNOSAURUS REX

T. rex. So famous it gets by with a first initial. *Tyrannosaurus rex,* whose name means "tyrant lizard king," might be the most famous of all dinosaurs. But why is "the king" so famous? First, it was very big—more than 40 feet (12 meters) long and weighing more than 7 tons (6.4 metric tons). Second, it was a fierce predator. A single bite from *Tyrannosaurus* would snap a lion or a grizzly bear in half. Finally, *Tyrannosaurus* is famous because it had a shape different from any animal living today.

No humans lived at the same time as *Tyrannosaurus,* so how do we know about this creature? We know about it because scientists have found and studied its fossils. Fossils are bones, teeth, footprints, and other remains that are preserved in rocks. Paleontologists—people who study fossils—use these remains to piece together the lives and habits of ancient creatures.

Usually, paleontologists don't start with a complete skeleton of a dinosaur. Instead, they study the animal rock by rock, bone by bone. And this is how we learned about *Tyrannosaurus.*

Just over a century ago, nobody knew a thing about *Tyrannosaurus rex.* Now practically everyone does. This is the story of the discoveries that helped us understand the tyrant lizard king.

Stonesfield, United Kingdom, and Barnsboro, New Jersey:
Giant Predatory Dinosaurs

1824

Reverend William Buckland, a paleontologist, officially states that the jawbone belonged to an animal called *Megalosaurus*, or "big lizard." Due to Buckland's description, people learn that giant reptilian predators once roamed the earth. Scientists still do not have enough bones to make a complete skeleton though. Buckland incorrectly assumes that *Megalosaurus* walked on all fours like today's lizards.

1797

An unnamed fossil collector finds a lower jawbone in a quarry in Stonesfield. The jawbone contains several large teeth that look like serrated knives.

William Buckland

1842
Paleontologist Sir Richard Owen coins the word dinosaur ("fearfully great lizard"). As the original three examples of dinosaurs, Owen lists *Megalosaurus* and the plant eaters *Iguanodon* and *Hylaeosaurus*.

Edward Drinker Cope

1866
In a pit near Barnsboro, New Jersey, fossil diggers find a jawbone, some vertebrae, arm bones, and leg bones. American paleontologist Edward Drinker Cope names this new carnivore *Laelaps*, after a Greek mythological dog that was frozen into stone mid-leap. The jaws and teeth of *Laelaps* are a lot like those of *Megalosaurus*. However, the difference between the very short arms and very long legs shows that *Laelaps*—and probably *Megalosaurus* too—walked on its hind legs, not on all fours.

1877
Cope's rival, paleontologist Othniel Charles Marsh, points out that the name *Laelaps* is already being used for something much smaller—a type of mite—so the dinosaur needs a new name. He changes *Laelaps* to *Dryptosaurus* ("wounding lizard").

Othniel Charles Marsh

an 1862 interpretation of what *Megalosaurus* may have looked like

Judith River, Montana; Garden Park Fossil Area, Colorado; and Drumheller, Alberta, Canada: *Flesh Eaters of the North American West*

Benjamin Mudge

1877
Geologist Benjamin Mudge, collecting for Othniel Marsh, discovers several bones of a Jurassic carnivorous dinosaur in Garden Park Fossil Area, Colorado. Marsh sees that the bones come from a new type of dinosaur, so he names it *Allosaurus* ("other lizard").

1856
Geologist and explorer Ferdinand Vandeveer Hayden discovers dinosaur teeth in Cretaceous rocks near the Judith River in today's Montana. He sends the teeth to paleontologist Joseph Leidy, who notices that some of the teeth are similar to those of *Megalosaurus*. He names the new creature *Deinodon* ("terrible tooth"). This is the first time that a scientist has recognized carnivorous dinosaur fossils in North America.

teeth of a carnivore

1883

Field collector Marshall P. Felch digs in a Jurassic-age Garden Park quarry. He makes two important discoveries of giant meat-eating dinosaurs. The first is a nearly complete skeleton of *Allosaurus*. The other is a horned creature, which Marsh names *Ceratosaurus* ("horned lizard"). These very complete skeletons prove that meat-eating dinosaurs were indeed two-legged animals with short arms.

Ceratosaurus

Tyrannosaurus rex skull

Joseph Burr Tyrrell

1884

Near Drumheller, in Alberta, Canada, geologist Joseph Burr Tyrrell finds a partial crushed skull of a large Cretaceous meat-eating dinosaur.

1892

Cope describes Tyrrell's skull as a part of *Laelaps*. (He refuses to use his rival Marsh's new name, *Dryptosaurus*.) The skull turns out to belong to a different meat eater. It is the first tyrant dinosaur skull ever found.

Golden, Colorado; Alkali Creek, Wyoming; and South Dakota:

Tyrannosaurus Lurks Unknown

John Bell Hatcher

1874

In Golden, Colorado, naturalist and teacher Arthur Lakes finds a giant tooth of a meat-eating dinosaur. He sends it to Othniel Marsh. Scientists won't know this for another 30 years, but *Tyrannosaurus* has been discovered!

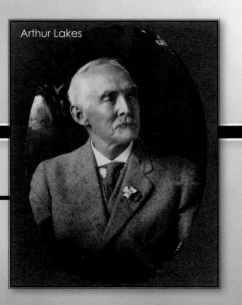

Arthur Lakes

1891

Paleontologist John Bell Hatcher, collecting for Marsh near Alkali Creek, finds the hind limb of a giant carnivorous dinosaur. Later, he and collector A. E. Sullins find hip bones of the same type of dinosaur. Marsh assigns these bones to a little-known collection of fossils that he is calling *Ornithomimus grandis*. It's later discovered that the bones belong to *Tyrannosaurus*.

1892

Collectors in South Dakota find a pair of large, badly weathered vertebrae. Cope believes they come from a new kind of horned dinosaur. He calls the creature *Manospondylus* ("spongy vertebrae"), due to the hollow, foamlike texture inside the bones. Scientists later discover that these bones also come from *Tyrannosaurus*.

T. rex attacking *Triceratops*

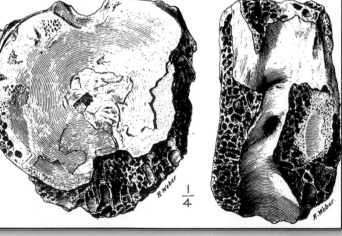

$\frac{1}{4}$

sketch of *Manospondylus* vertebrae

1896

Marsh writes a big book about the dinosaurs of North America. In the book he correctly guesses that *Ornithomimus grandis* (*Tyrannosaurus*) was "one of the most destructive enemies" of *Triceratops* and the other horned dinosaurs.

Sevenmile Creek, Wyoming; Jordan, Montana; and Dry Creek, Montana:
The Tyrant King Emerges!

Barnum Brown studying fossils in 1933

1900

In northeastern Wyoming, paleontologist Barnum Brown is fossil hunting for Henry Fairfield Osborn of the American Museum of Natural History in New York. Brown finds a partial skeleton of a gigantic carnivorous dinosaur much larger than any found before.

American Museum of Natural History, New York, circa 1900

1902

In Jordan, Montana, Brown discovers another partial skeleton of the same species.

1905

Osborn decides that Brown's skeletons come from two different species: *Dynamosaurus imperiosus* ("commanding dynamic lizard") and *Tyrannosaurus rex* ("tyrant lizard king"). He believes these species to be much bigger than *Megalosaurus*, *Dryptosaurus*, *Allosaurus*, and *Ceratosaurus*.

Osborn renames the 1884 Drumheller skulls that Cope named *Laelaps*. He calls them *Albertosaurus* after the Canadian province of Alberta. Osborn realizes that *Albertosaurus* is a very close relative of *Tyrannosaurus*.

early drawing of *T. rex*

American Museum of Natural History *T. rex* mount, 1915

1915

The 1908 specimen is mounted for display. This version of *Tyrannosaurus* becomes one of the most famous dinosaur skeletons ever. It is later used for the *Jurassic Park* logo. (However, based on what we know today, the mounting has many errors: it is dragging its tail; it is standing too upright; and its hands have three fingers instead of two.)

1906

Osborn realizes that he made a mistake. Brown's 1900 and 1902 skeletons are both *Tyrannosaurus*. He also coins the name Tyrannosauridae for the family of tyrant dinosaurs.

1908

Brown finds an even more complete skeleton of *Tyrannosaurus* in Montana.

Carter County and Jordan, Montana:
Dwarf Tyrants or Young Tyrannosaurus?

Harley Garbani

1942
Paleontologist David H. Dunkle finds a nearly complete skull of a small tyrant dinosaur in Carter County, Montana.

1946
Smithsonian paleontologist Charles W. Gilmore claims that Dunkle's skull comes from a new species of tyrant dinosaur, *Gorgosaurus*.

skull found by David Dunkle

1969
In Jordan, Montana, fossil collector Harley Garbani finds a partial skull of a small carnivorous dinosaur and a partial skeleton of a medium-sized one.

T. rex on display at the Natural History Museum of Los Angeles County

EXPERT: *Thomas Carr*

Thomas Carr (born in 1968) is a paleontologist from Toronto, Canada. He is an expert on *Tyrannosaurus* and other tyrant dinosaurs. As a college student at York University and the University of Toronto, he studied how tyrant dinosaurs grow. Today he teaches at Carthage College in Wisconsin. He is also the director of the Dinosaur Discovery Museum.

Carr discovered and named three types of tyrant dinosaurs: *Appalachiosaurus*, *Bistahieversor*, and *Teratophoneus*. He also showed that the skull of a creature once called *Nanotyrannus* is almost certainly a young *Tyrannosaurus*.

Carr is a good scientist because he is a detailed observer and he describes his observations clearly. For instance, he has made very detailed observations on the bones of tyrant dinosaurs. He has discovered many reasons why the same bone in two different dinosaurs could be different. The dinosaurs might be different ages, different genders (male or female), or different species. Or there might just be individual differences that make every dinosaur unique.

1999
Paleontologist Thomas Carr shows that Dunkle's skull comes from a young animal, not a fully grown one. It is almost certainly a young *Tyrannosaurus*.

1988
A team led by paleontologists Robert T. Bakker and Philip J. Currie describes Dunkle's skull. They believe it comes from a creature that they name *Nanotyrannus* ("dwarf tyrant").

2004
Carr and paleontologist Thomas Williamson show that the Garbani specimens are also young *Tyrannosaurus* specimens, not new tyrant dinosaurs. Scientists now know much more about the growth of *Tyrannosaurus* than they know about the growth of most other dinosaurs.

Ömnögovi, Mongolia, and Zhucheng, China: *Asian Cousins*

1955
Paleontologist Evgeny Maleev describes the fossils from Mongolia. He thinks that the biggest ones are actually from *Tyrannosaurus* and the smallest ones are from *Gorgosaurus*. He names the medium-sized skeletons *Tarbosaurus* ("terror lizard").

1946
In Mongolia, Soviet paleontologists find many fossils of a giant tyrant dinosaur nearly as big as *Tyrannosaurus*.

Tarbosaurus skull

1965

Paleontologist Anatoly K. Rozhdestvensky studies Maleev's specimens. He shows that they are the same species but in different growth stages. Some paleontologists consider them an Asian species of *Tyrannosaurus*, but most agree that *Tarbosaurus* is the proper name. In the next several decades, many more skeletons of *Tarbosaurus* are found.

Zhuchengtyrannus and offspring

construction of *Tarbosaurus* display in Singapore

2011

Paleontologist David Hone and colleagues describe fossils found near Zhucheng, China. They come from a creature closely related to *Tarbosaurus* and *Tyrannosaurus*. Hone names it *Zhuchengtyrannus* ("tyrant of Zhucheng").

ort Peck Lake, Montana: *The Nation's T. rex and a Girl named Bob*

T. rex in front of Museum of the Rockies

2000

Paleontologist Bob Harmon finds a partial *Tyrannosaurus* skeleton in the same general area. It gets the nickname "Bob."

1988

On a family camping trip to Fort Peck Lake, rancher Kathy Wankel discovers a few bones. She returns later to dig up some more bones. Then she takes them to paleontologist Jack Horner at the Museum of the Rockies in Bozeman, Montana.

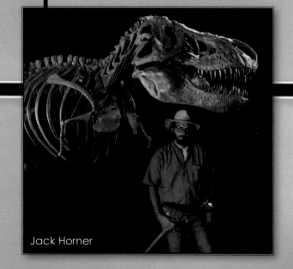

Jack Horner

1990

Crews from the Museum of the Rockies dig up the skeleton that Wankel found. At the time, it is the world's most complete *Tyrannosaurus*. It is also the first skeleton with a nearly complete arm.

femur of the Nation's *T. rex* being revealed at the Smithsonian Institution

2005
Paleontologist Mary Schweitzer and her team find a special type of bone tissue on the inside of Bob's thighbone. This type of tissue is only found in female birds and crocodilians when they are about to lay eggs. It is never in males. So, it turns out that Bob is a girl!

2014
Wankel's *Tyrannosaurus* gets transferred to the Smithsonian Institution in Washington, D.C. Because the Smithsonian is the national museum of the United States, this dinosaur's nickname is "the Nation's *T. rex*."

Near Faith, South Dakota: *Good Old Sue*

1992
Due to legal problems, Sue is taken from the Black Hills Institute until a judge can decide who actually owns the specimen.

Peter Larson with *Tyrannosaurus* skull

August 12, 1990
Amateur fossil hunter Susan Hendrickson sees the teeth and bones of a *Tyrannosaurus* sticking out of a hillside on the ranch of Maurice Williams.

teeth of Sue the *T. rex*

August 14–September 1, 1990
A team led by Peter Larson of the Black Hills Institute uncovers the skeleton. They name the dinosaur "Sue" in honor of Hendrickson. This is by far the most complete *Tyrannosaurus* ever found. It is also the largest, at 41 feet (12.5 m) long.

1997

Sue goes to auction, and the Field Museum of Natural History in Chicago wins her.

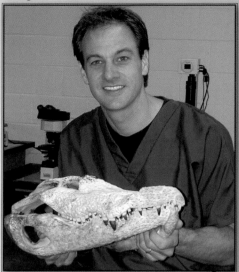

Greg Erickson

Sue on display at the Field Museum

2004

Paleontologist Greg Erickson and colleagues develop a new way to figure out a dinosaur's age at the time of its death. Sue turns out to be the oldest *Tyrannosaurus* they studied, at age 28. Erickson also found that *Tyrannosaurus* reached full size around age 18.

Eastend, Saskatchewan, Canada; Dry Creek, Montana; Jordan, Montana; and Harding County, South Dakota:

Traces of Tyrannosaurus Behavior

Karen Chin with coprolite samples

2000
Paleontologist Ken Carpenter examines an *Edmontosaurus* skeleton from Dry Creek, Montana. He shows that its tail bones were crushed and bitten off, probably by a *Tyrannosaurus*. The bones had healed. That meant the duckbill dinosaur had managed to escape the attack.

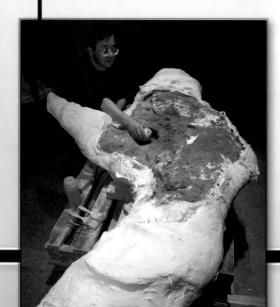

Ken Carpenter placing an orange at the eye position of a *Triceratops* skull

1998
Paleontologist Karen Chin and colleagues describe some *Tyrannosaurus* coprolite (fossilized dung) found in Eastend, Saskatchewan. It contains the partially digested and crunched bones of young plant-eating dinosaurs. This confirms that tyrant dinosaur bites were strong enough to crunch bones.

T. rex with kill

2005

Paleontologist John Happ studies a partial *Triceratops* skull found near Jordan. He observes that one of the horns was bitten off by a *Tyrannosaurus* but then healed. This discovery shows that *Tyrannosaurus* and *Triceratops* did fight each other—proving Marsh's 1896 theory.

T. rex attacking Edmontosaurus

2013

Paleontologist Robert DePalma and colleagues describe a series of *Edmontosaurus* fossils from Harding County showing healed bite wounds from *Tyrannosaurus*. The fossils include a skull with healed tooth gouges, duckbill skin with healed tooth punctures, and a tail vertebra with the broken tip of a *Tyrannosaurus* tooth still in it.

Ekalaka, Montana: *Jane, the Long-Legged Youngster*

Jane on display

2005
A special exhibit is held to show off the 21-foot (6.4-m) long skeleton. Compared to fully grown tyrants, Jane has long and slender legs, and she has more (but smaller) teeth. Tyrant dinosaur experts from all over the world attend a conference in honor of Jane. Some paleontologists (such as Bakker, Currie, and Larson) are convinced that Jane is a complete *Nanotyrannus*. Others (such as Carr, Williamson, and this author) believe Jane is a young *Tyrannosaurus*.

2001
Fossil hunters Carol Tuck and Bill Harrison find a skeleton of a medium-sized meat-eating dinosaur near Ekalaka. It turns out to be a nearly complete skeleton, nicknamed "Jane" (even though the animal's gender is unknown).

2004
Greg Erickson and colleagues figure out that Jane was only 11 years old when she died.

two tyrannosaurs at battle

2009

Paleontologist Joseph Peterson and colleagues describe bite marks on Jane's face. The marks closely match the shape of Jane's own teeth. The bites healed, so they weren't fatal. This shows that young tyrants bit each other in the face, perhaps when fighting over food.

Lujiatun, Wucaiwan, and Batuyingzi, China: *Feathered, Long-Armed Ancestors*

Xu Xing

2004

A team led by paleontologist Xu Xing describes a tiny, 4-foot- (1.2-m-) long tyrant dinosaur from Cretaceous rocks of northeastern China. They name it *Dilong* ("emperor dragon"). This site in Lujiatun is famous for preserving animal feathers, fur, and other body coverings. (Most rocks do not do this.) *Dilong* had a fuzzy body covering. Paleontologists predicted that this covering would be present in other tyrant dinosaurs as well.

Dilongs with brachiosaurs

Yutyrannus

2012

Private collectors find three nearly complete skeletons of primitive tyrant dinosaurs from Cretaceous rocks of Batuyingzi, China. Like the other primitive tyrants, they had three-fingered hands. They were also covered with long, slender feathers. This shows that even big tyrants—perhaps even *Tyrannosaurus*—were feathered. Xu Xing and colleagues named this dinosaur *Yutyrannus* ("feathered tyrant").

2005

In Wucaiwan, China, Xu and colleagues find several Jurassic-age specimens, including a nearly complete adult skull and a complete juvenile skeleton of a primitive tyrant dinosaur.

2006

Xu and colleagues name this new discovery *Guanlong* ("crowned dragon") because it has a tall head crest. They show that *Guanlong* was a very early tyrant dinosaur with long arms with three grasping fingers. It was less than 12 feet (3.7 m) long.

About *Tyrannosaurus*

Length: 41 feet (12.5 m)

Height: 13 feet (4 m) at the hips

Weight: more than 7 tons (6.4 metric tons)

Age: 67 to 66 million years ago (end of Cretaceous Period)

Location: Western North America

Diet: Meat, especially other dinosaurs. Bite marks confirm that they fed on the duckbill dinosaur *Edmontosaurus* and the horned dinosaur *Triceratops*, but probably all dinosaurs in its environment were on the menu.

Lifespan: 30 years or so. Full size is reached at around age 18.

Distinctive features: Tiny arms ending in two fingers (unlike some other tyrants, which had three). Skull with rounded snout and expanded back, giving forward-pointing vision. Adult *Tyrannosaurus* had fewer teeth than most flesh-eating dinosaurs (as few as 15 in the upper jaw and 13 in the lower), but the teeth were extremely large (up to 12 inches/30.5 centimeters long, including the root).

Enemies: The main enemy of *Tyrannosaurus* was its own kind. As young animals, however, they might be eaten by crocodilians and the dinosaur *Acheroraptor*. Also, they might be injured if an *Edmontosaurus*, *Triceratops*, or armored *Ankylosaurus* or *Denversaurus* fought back.

Glossary

amateur—someone who does something as a hobby rather than a profession

carnivore—an animal that eats meat

Cretaceous Period—the span of geologic time from 145 to 66 million years ago; the third of three geologic periods from the Mesozoic Era

fossil—the remains of a living thing (like bones and teeth) or traces of its action (like footprints) preserved in the rock record; evidence of life from the geologic past

geologist—a scientist who studies minerals, rocks, and soil

paleontologist—a scientist who studies fossils

predator—an animal that hunts other animals for food

quarry—a place where stone or other minerals are dug from the ground

species—a particular kind of living thing

specimen—a particular individual or sample of something; in fossils, a specimen is the remains of one particular example of a species

theory—an idea that explains something that is unknown

tissue—a layer or bunch of soft material that makes up body parts

tyrant—a cruel ruler

vertebra—a back bone; more than one vertebra are vertebrae

Read More

Bakker, Robert T., and Luis V. Rey (illus.). *The Big Golden Book of Dinosaurs*. New York: Golden Book, 2013.

Brusatte, Steve. *Field Guide to Dinosaurs*. New York: Book Sales Inc., 2009.

Holtz Jr., Thomas R. *Dinosaurs: The Most Complete, Up-to-Date Encyclopedia for Dinosaur Lovers of All Ages*. New York: Random House, 2007.

McCurry, Kristen, and Juan Calle (illus.). *How to Draw Incredible Dinosaurs*. North Mankato, Minn.: Capstone Press, 2013.

Internet Sites

Use FactHound to find Internet sites related to this book. All of the sites on FactHound have been researched by our staff.

Here's all you do:

Visit www.facthound.com

Type in this code: 9781491421253

ABOUT THE AUTHOR

Thomas R. Holtz Jr. is a vertebrate paleontologist with the University of Maryland Department of Geology. He has authored dozens of books and articles on dinosaurs for children and adults. He has even appeared in dinosaur-themed comic strips. A graduate of Yale and Johns Hopkins, Dr. Holtz lives in Maryland when he's not traveling the world, hunting fossils.

Index

Bibliography

Brochu, C.A. 2003. Osteology of *Tyrannosaurus rex*: insights from a nearly complete skeleton and high-resolution computed tomographic analysis of the skull. *Journal of Vertebrate Paleontology* 22 (Suppl. To 4): 1–138. DOI: 10.1080/02724634.2003.10010947.

Carpenter, K. 2000. Evidence of predatory behavior by carnivorous dinosaurs. *Gaia* 15: 135–144.

Carr, T.D. 1999. Craniofacial ontogeny in Tyrannosauridae (Dinosauria: Coelurosauria.) *Journal of Vertebrate Paleontology* 19: 497–520. doi: 10.1080/02724634.1999.10011161.

Carr, T.D. & T.E. Williamson. 2004. Diversity of late Maastrichtian Tyrannosauridae (Dinosauria: Theropoda) from western North America. *Zoological Journal of the Linnean Society* 142: 479–523. DOI: 10.1111/j.1096-3642.2004.00130.x.

Gilmore, C.W. 1920. Osteology of the carnivorous Dinosauria in the United States National Museum, with special reference to the genera *Antrodemus (Allosaurus)* and *Ceratosaurus*. *Bulletin of the United States National Museum* 110: 1–154. DOI: 10.5479/si.03629236.110.

Horner, J.R. & D. Lessem. 1993. *The Complete T. rex: How Stunning New Discoveries are Changing Our Understanding of the World's Most Famous Dinosaur.* Simon & Schuster. 239 pp.

Larson, P.L. & K. Carpenter (eds). 2008. *Tyrannosaurus rex, the Tyrant King.* Indiana Univ. Press. 456 pp.

Marsh, O.C. 1896. The dinosaurs of North America. *Annual Report of the US Geological Survey* 16: 133–414.

Osborn, H.F. 1917. Skeletal adaptations of *Ornitholestes, Struthiomimus, Tyrannosaurus. Bulletin of the American Museum of Natural History* 35: 733–771.

Parrish, J.M.; R.E. Molnar; P.J. Currie & E.B. Koppelhus (eds). 2013. *Tyrannosaurid Paleobiology.* Indiana Univ. Press. 312 pp.

Peterson, J.E.; M.D. Henderson; R.P. Scherer & C.P. Vittore. 2009. Face biting on a juvenile tyrannosaurid and behavioral implications. *Palaios* 24: 780–784. Doi: 10.2110/palo.2009.p09-056r.

Tanke, D.H. & K. Carpenter. 2001. *Mesozoic Vertebrate Life: New Research Inspired by the Paleontology of Philip J. Currie.* Indiana Univ. Press. 352 pp.